Original title:
50 Shades of Life's Uncertainty

Copyright © 2025 Creative Arts Management OÜ
All rights reserved.

Author: Julian Montgomery
ISBN HARDBACK: 978-1-80566-100-9
ISBN PAPERBACK: 978-1-80566-395-9

Notes from the Edge of Time

In a world where plans go south,
And socks lose their partners, no doubt,
We dance in circles, a little absurd,
Chasing dreams while life sings the unheard.

Sometimes the rain makes us wear frowns,
Other times, it's just puddles for clowns,
We juggle quite well, our hopes on a string,
Life's a circus, come join in the swing!

With breakfast burnt and coffee gone cold,
Life's little mishaps never get old,
Yet laughter erupts from chaos we find,
A ticklish giggle in the back of the mind.

So bring on the whimsy, the silly, the fun,
In this topsy-turvy race we all run,
For every stumble has a spark of delight,
As we march on ahead, despite the weird fright!

Glimmers amidst the Gloom

In the morning, what a sight,
Coffee spills, but that's alright.
Socks mismatched, a brand new start,
Laughter bubbles, warms the heart.

Umbrellas flip, it starts to pour,
Out the door, we dance and roar.
Life's a joke, sometimes a riddle,
Grab a friend, play them the fiddle.

Threads of the Uncertain Weave

Knitting chaos, thread tangles tight,
Patterns shifting, none feel right.
But every stitch, a smile in disguise,
Who needs plans when we improvise?

Buttons misplaced, an awkward dress,
Fashion police, we must confess.
Yet with each twist, a tale we spin,
Life's a quilt, we laugh, we grin.

Sonic Waves of Possibility

Tuning forks, they sing off-key,
Dancing notes, wild and free.
The radio glitches, joy we find,
Groovy beats leave worries behind.

Disco lights in the living room,
We twirl around, chasing the gloom.
Each misstep is a chance to shine,
Life's a concert, all's divine.

The Struggle of Certitudes

Plans set in stone, but here they bend,
Schedules clash, will this ever end?
Yet through the mess, we find our way,
Let's flip the script, it's a comedy play.

Life's wild ride, a bumpy course,
In each pothole, there's hidden force.
So grab your hat, embrace the fun,
In the absurdity, we've already won.

Whispers of the Unknown

What's for dinner? A mystery feast,
Five-star chef or maybe just yeast.
My socks don't match, it's a fashion crime,
But who needs style when you're out of time?

Life's a riddle, a puzzle to solve,
I ask for help, but how can I evolve?
The cat's in charge, plotting my doom,
While I search for sanity in this small room.

The Colors of Ambiguity

I bought a paint, but it's not quite blue,
Is it green, or just a splash of dew?
When asked my age, I play the coy,
Just a number, like my strange new toy.

With mixed signals, like dishes I bake,
One's a treat, and the other—oops, a mistake!
Life's a box of chocolates all around,
One bite sweet, the next can astound.

Treading the Tightrope

I walk the line, a circus act,
Balancing snacks and a late-night snack.
With each step, I'm a thimble in fates,
Dodging life's pies and the slippery plates.

The gym? Oh please, my couch is just fine,
A marathon of shows gives me plenty of time.
Each decision a dance, a waltz of sorts,
Watch me trip, as chaos reports!

Shadows in the Sunlight

I plan a trip, but the sun goes away,
The weatherman laughs as I rue the day.
A suitcase packed with nothing but dreams,
Reality kicks, or so it seems.

Every shadow holds secrets untold,
In the sunlight, my plans feel bold.
Yet here I stand, with ice cream in hand,
Savoring moments, as best as I can.

The Dance of Doubt

In the ballroom of choices, we sway and spin,
Yet every step makes me question, where to begin.
The music's a riddle, the tune's out of sight,
With each awkward shuffle, it feels so not right.

My partner just giggles, but it's hard to believe,
With two left feet, could we ever achieve?
We giggle and wobble, our confidence frail,
But we'll dance until dawn, through a comic detail.

Layers of the Unseen

Peeling back layers to find what is true,
Turns out there's spring onions, not just a shoe.
With each new discovery comes laughter and frowns,
What's hidden beneath brings both smiles and some frowns.

A sock and a pickle, what a curious pair,
Life's like a riddle, full of surprises to share.
We laugh at the chaos, embrace every twist,
For in layers of nonsense, it's joy that persists.

Echoes of What Might Be

In a hall of reflections, I hear echoes loud,
Of choices I ponder while feeling quite proud.
"Is it green eggs or ham?" I ponder and muse,
While wrestling my worries with colorful views.

The echoes just giggle, with whispers so sly,
And I chase the shadows of things passing by.
What if I jump? What if I stay?
In the comedy of life, I laugh all the way.

Chasing Elusive Dreams

With a net made of wishes, I chase dreams like bees,
They flit and they flutter, just out of my reach.
I trip over sneakers and tumble with style,
As I fumble for futures that make me compile.

Every wild notion darts off with a grin,
Leaving me gasping, "Can I even begin?"
But the chase is a dance, though riddled with glee,
In the funny pursuit of what's hoping to be.

The Interplay of Fear and Freedom

In the dance of choices, we trip and slide,
Making plans while seeking a place to hide.
A leap of faith, or just a bound of doubt?
Is the exit here, or just a crazy route?

With nerves like cats, we prowl the night,
Chasing dreams that glimmer, or staying tight.
A parachute made from a silk tie,
Who knew fashion could make a bold guy fly?

Seeds of Potential in a Wild Garden

In a patch of chaos, we plant our dreams,
Watering doubts with self-sabotage screams.
Weeds of worry sprout, seeking the sun,
While blooming joy's petals blur the fun.

A garden of giggles, grown under a frown,
Where daisies wear sunglasses and tulips all clown.
Every plant's a question, growing in sight,
Do they bloom for the day, or dance in the night?

Unveiling the Canvas of Chance

With a brush of whimsy, we smear the fate,
Mixing hues of nonsense on a wobbly plate.
A splash of fortune, a dash of fear,
Creating a masterpiece that's never quite clear.

Each stroke a giggle, each smudge a sigh,
It's a joyous riddle, oh me, oh my!
Should we frame this chaos or toss it away?
Art's just like life—who knows what will stay?

Questions in the Quiet

In the silence whispers, doubts softly creep,
Like mice in the pantry, stealing our sleep.
Do we chase the answers or savor the snack,
In the stillness of moments, why do we lack?

With thoughts like popcorn, they pop and bounce,
Should we dance to the rhythm, or merely renounce?
Each query a riddle, wrapped tight in dreams,
Searching for laughter in the hush of moonbeams.

Pages of a Perpetual Mystery

Every morning brings a giggle,
With toast that just won't wiggle.
The coffee spills, the cat won't play,
Yet somehow brightens up the day.

A sock misses its perfect pair,
As I ponder life's petty flare.
The bus is late, what a surprise,
But hey, at least I'm still alive!

The mailman's dancing down the street,
With packages for whom? Not me, sweet!
I wave as he prances by with glee,
In this odd ballet, joy's key.

So open a page, take a peek,
What quirkiness shall spring this week?
The adventures of life, absurdly spun,
Just laugh along, and have some fun!

Embracing the Uninvited

A knock at the door, who could it be?
An unexpected guest, oh dear, oh me!
With snacks unprepared and chaos ahead,
We'll make it a party, let go of dread!

The weather report says expect snow,
Yet here I am, in shorts, ready to go!
Umbrellas parade, while flip-flops cheer,
In this wacky dance, joy is near.

A cook's surprise, nothing quite devout,
Gourmet burnt toast? What's that about?
Laughter erupts, and we all take a bite,
Life's little mishaps make everything right.

So bring on the uninvited foes,
A whirlwind of mayhem, that's how it flows.
With smiles and jokes and hearts all laid bare,
We'll embrace the confusion with flamboyant flair!

The Allure of Indefiniteness

A riddle wrapped in a puzzling tune,
Just like my cat lost in the afternoon.
Where's that last piece of the jigsaw gone?
Oh, there it is, right on the lawn!

Plans made yesterday, where did they go?
The world spins wildly—what a show!
I marked my birthday, but missed the date,
Whoops! Just a reason to celebrate!

Mysteries bubble like fizzy drinks,
With every wrong turn, my heart winks.
The universe giggles at my grand scheme,
As life leads me down paths that gleam.

So here's to the charm of never knowing,
Like a surprise party that's always showing.
Embrace the chaos, the leap into space,
In this wild dance, we find our place!

Ascent through Uncertainty

Up the stairs of a rickety house,
Where a surprise waits, quiet as a mouse.
The light flickers, and what do I find?
A joyous mess of life's sweet grind.

A recipe calls for eggs and some flair,
But all that I have is a clueless stare.
With random ingredients, a dish will rise,
Confidence brewing in novice guise.

A hike in the woods, where paths intertwine,
Each twist and turn is a glass of fine wine.
The squirrel's confused, which way to skitter?
But that makes the journey all the glitter!

So step boldly forth, with laughter and cheer,
Unlock the doors of whimsy, my dear.
In life's big adventure, take the chance,
For uncertainty leads to the best romance!

Threads of Fate

In a world of tangled strings,
We dance like puppets on a whim.
Life hands us choices with a grin,
We might just trip, or learn to swim.

Fortune cookies crack, we chuckle,
Predictions made by slip of tongue.
Yet here we are, in this great shuffle,
With every mistake, more songs are sung.

The Swirl of Hesitation

In the land of might-have-beens,
I flip a coin, either way I spin.
Should I wear a hat or just wear jeans?
Life's just one big game of din.

I ponder long and let it linger,
Gossip flows like water from a sink.
Do I choose the spicy or the finger?
One's a bite, the other's a drink.

Beyond the Horizon's Veil

I peep through clouds, what lies beyond?
A chance for laughter or a serious bond?
The sun peeks out, like a cheeky frond,
Mistakes are like jellybeans, tasty yet conned.

Onward I march, with my mismatched shoes,
Each step I take, I might just snooze.
The future's a riddle, a cryptic muse,
In the waiting game, who'll pay their dues?

Labors of a Wandering Heart

My heart's a map with scribbles and stains,
It flits around like a runaway train.
Am I lost or napping on this plane?
Love's a puzzle, with missing frames.

I ask the stars for a hint or two,
They wink back like they really knew.
Is love a dance or a wild zoo?
A circus act with no clear view.

Possibilities in the Dark

In shadows where the outcomes play,
A game of hide and seek each day.
With every twist and little turn,
I ponder things I'll never learn.

A cat might land on its feet right,
But I just trip and lose my sight.
In darkness, jokes are extra bright,
Creating laughs to ease the fright.

Embracing the Unpredictable

The weather's mood, its whimsy spins,
Like rollercoasters, ups and grins.
A coffee spill, a burst of glee,
Life's comedy is wild and free.

Expect the worst? You might just find,
A puppy dance to ease your mind.
With every hiccup, laugh it off,
After all, who needs a scoff?

The Weight of Every Choice

A fork in roads, I sense the fun,
Which way to go? Oh, it's a run!
A salad bowl or fries instead,
Will shape my fate and fill my head.

Each decision wears a heavy hat,
Like trying to catch a wily cat.
With every slip, there's giggle gleam,
Unraveling a silly dream.

Unfolding in Mysterious Ways

Life's surprises, twists and turns,
Offer treasures, if one learns.
A lost sock's tale in the breeze,
Might just inspire, oh yes please!

Unexpected bumps along the street,
Can lead to adventures, oh so sweet.
Each moment's zany, fresh, and new,
Like wearing mismatched shoes, who knew?

Between the Lines of Certainty

I bought a crystal ball, you see,
It told me things would never be.
But then it cracked, the truth's absurd,
Now I just chase my flying bird.

Plans are like socks, they lost a pair,
One's in the wash, one's in the air.
I scribble notes that go unread,
And hope for lunch instead of dread.

I thought I'd find the path to gold,
But really, I'm just a bit too bold.
Life's a game where rules are fake,
I laughed so hard, I spilled my cake.

So here I sit, a jester's grin,
In life's big circus, let the fun begin.
With every twist and every turn,
I learn again, and still I yearn.

The Spectrum of What-Ifs

What if I wore a clown's bright shoes?
What if I danced without a cue?
What if the sun turned into cheese?
I'd juggle moonbeams, if you please.

What if the wind decided to sing?
What if I found a lost gold ring?
What if the cat could play guitar?
I'd host a show and make her a star.

What if a cupcake flew up high?
What if it lands and says goodbye?
What if the sky just flipped around?
I'd try to catch it, safe and sound.

What if my dreams don't make the cut?
I'd laugh it off, stay in my rut.
For every 'what-if' that fills my head,
I'll spin a tale, no need for dread.

Tides of Change and Chance

The tide came in, my boat went out,
I waved a flag, but there's no doubt.
I built a castle, it washed away,
Next time, I'll use marshmallows for play.

With every wave, a new surprise,
I dance with crabs underneath the skies.
The shells I gather tell strange tales,
Of pirate gold and slippery snails.

What if the moon becomes a peach?
What if the stars were within reach?
I'll sail my raft on dreams tonight,
With jellyfish as my guiding light.

But as I float on whims of fate,
I laugh aloud, uncertainty's great!
For every wave that pulls me near,
I just might catch a cozy cheer.

Fading Footprints in the Sand

I walked the shore, my footprints bold,
But then they vanished, truth be told.
The tide liked them a little too much,
Just like my plans on evening's hush.

I scribbled secrets in the sand,
But then a seagull came and planned.
It stole my thoughts and flew away,
Now I just talk to shells all day.

What if the ocean spoke to me?
What if it said, 'Just let it be?'
I'd trade my worries, I'd trade my sway,
For laughter and tides that laugh and play.

In shifting sands, I'll find my way,
With every giggle, come what may.
For in each wave that breaks and bends,
Life's simply fun, and never ends.

Whispers in the Fog

In the mist, my socks mispair,
Lost in thought, but not despair.
Dancing shadows play a tune,
Is it Tuesday, or is it June?

Coffee spills in weird locations,
Hot debates with moth creations.
Life's a riddle, wrapped in jest,
A guessing game, at best, at best!

Waiting for a knock at one,
Hope it's joy, not just the sun.
Sidewalk cracks that lead to dreams,
Or maybe just my childhood schemes.

So here we stand, a playful lot,
Amidst the fog, a silly plot.
Finding giggles in the haze,
Oh, life, you funny, baffling maze!

The Palette of Possibility

With colors bright, I paint my day,
But water spills in a funny way.
Cyan skies and emerald grass,
Do I need classes, or just a glass?

Brushes slip, and paint goes wide,
A masterpiece? Or a lovely slide?
Swirling hues of wild delight,
Like sprinkles on a cupcake fight.

A canvas blank does look so lame,
Yet mishaps yield the best of fame.
Splattered hues tell stories bold,
Each drip a treasure to behold.

So here I sit, in paint-spattered glee,
Creating chaos, it's just me!
Laughing at the mess I wield,
The palette's secrets now revealed!

Threads of Unraveling

A tangled yarn beneath the chair,
Knots and loops, a crafty affair.
Purls and stitches, all in fun,
But where'd I put my other gun?

With needles flying, bright yarns clash,
Creating something from a dash.
But oh! What's this? A sock gone rogue,
Or a scarf that started on the Oge?

Life's a quilt of odd designs,
Misplaced buttons, broken lines.
Each thread a giggle, each tear a smile,
Let's embrace the crazy, if just for a while.

So sit with me in this fabric mess,
In stitches, we'll find happiness.
With threads unwoven, tales to share,
Life's a cozy, chaotic air!

Shadows Beneath the Surface

In puddles deep, reflections swirl,
Is that my hat? Or just a whirl?
Monsters hide in watery dreams,
Planning schemes with silly beams.

The shadows dance as raindrops play,
A game of hide and seek they say.
With every splash, a chuckle's bred,
Even the fish have thoughts to spread.

Beneath the waves, a world unspooled,
Where jellybeans and laughter ruled.
Swirling tides, a merry twist,
Life's a joke, we can't resist.

So let's dive down, explore the fun,
In shadowed realms 'til day is done.
With giggles echoing in the deep,
We'll cherish secrets that we keep!

Highlights in the Abyss

Falling in and out of luck,
What's next? A dancing duck!
Juggling dreams and soggy fries,
Finding meaning in the pies.

Life's a trip, a wild ride,
Where logic often tries to hide.
Frogs in hats and cats that sing,
Embracing chaos is the thing!

Worry not; wear mismatched socks,
Ghosts pop in for paradox talks.
Each twist and turn, a cozy jest,
Who knew the abyss was a fest?

With every laugh, a spark ignites,
In darkness, we're the shining lights.
So grab a clown nose, join the dance,
Life's absurd, just take a chance!

Dreams Adrift on the Sea of Anxiety

Sailing boats of cotton candy,
Where every wave feels just so dandy.
With seagulls quacking silly rhymes,
Life's a farce with shared punchlines.

Riding high on whimsy's tide,
Where every worry takes a slide.
Paddling with a floaty duck,
Oh look, a fortune cookie stuck!

Fish with dreams of becoming stars,
Dance with joy beneath the bars.
With every splash of salty cheer,
I find my truth within the fear.

Laughter fills the ocean's blue,
A treasure map, just follow through.
Though storms may come, my heart is free,
On this ride, just let it be!

Choose Your Own Adventure

Turn the page or take a pause,
Life's a book without a cause.
With choices that twist like a straw,
Every chapter breaks a law.

Will I parry with a llama?
Or ride a scooter on a drama?
A taco truck or dragon fight,
Each decision feels so right.

Caped crusaders in pajamas,
Packet of chips or wild bananas?
Slide into joy, leap over strife,
In this novel, I'm the life!

Page by page, I'll write my fate,
In laughter, I shall celebrate.
A ludicrous tale, that's what I'll weave,
In the story of what I believe!

Dancing on the Tightrope of Fate

With a tutu made of pizza crust,
I balance on the whims of trust.
The audience throws jellybeans,
I pirouette in my wild dreams.

A stilt-walker with rubber ducks,
The tightrope sways with giggling luck.
Each wobble sparks a fit of glee,
As fate plays tricks, just wait and see!

A tumble down, a graceful fall,
"Hello, world!" I'll humorously call.
With every slip, I find my groove,
In absurdity, my heart will move.

So join the dance, let's take the chance,
Life's a circus, let's do the prance!
In the balance of chaos, with hope,
We'll laugh along the tightrope's slope!

A Palette of Possibilities

In colors bright, chaos swirls,
With every brush, a new mishmash twirls.
I paint my hopes with shades of glee,
But get splotches on my cup of tea.

Today it's red, tomorrow's blue,
I mix them up, then spill on my shoe.
Life's canvas, oh, a joyous mess,
I laugh at my art; who could guess?

With splatters bold, I twirl and dip,
A masterpiece from my chaotic trip.
Yet what's the theme? I hardly know,
But who needs plans when you can glow?

So grab your paints, don't be shy,
Life's answered with a wink and a pie.
Through every blunder, we still thrive,
In this zany swirl, we find our drive.

The Fog of Tomorrow

Through mist so thick, what do I see?
A dance of doubt, just watching me.
Is that a path, or did I snag?
Wait, was that a cat or just a rag?

Tomorrow's news, it feels so vague,
Like guessing right in a game of tag.
Do I wear shades or a raincoat now?
The forecast says, "Just wing it, wow!"

A foggy dance, I spin around,
Searching for clarity, which cannot be found.
But I trip on a rock, oh what a show!
Coughing mist, I giggle low.

So here's my motto, clear or blurred,
Embrace the silly, don't be deterred.
Tomorrow's fog may cloud my view,
But who needs light when laughter's true?

Fragments of a Flickering Future

Bits of sparkle dance in air,
Flickers of dreams, do I dare?
Will my plans bloom or turn to dust?
Can I even bench press my own trust?

Each fragile thought, a puzzle piece,
As I scramble around for inner peace.
Will I rise up like toast, or flop?
A decision's looming, but will I stop?

A future bright, or just a bluff?
With glittery doubts, it's getting tough.
I flip my coin, fate on display,
Heads or tails? Just another day!

With laughable odds, I roll the dice,
What's in store, life's secret spice?
Come what may, I'll take a chance,
In this flickering world, I'll dance!

Navigating the Gray

In shades of gray, I steer my boat,
Through waves of doubt, I hope to float.
Is that a storm, or just a breeze?
I'll pack my snacks, I aim to please.

With charts and maps, I plot my way,
But who knows what waits in the sway?
A seagull squawks, "Trust the unknown!"
I shout back, "But I'm all alone!"

Yet laughter echoes across the tide,
As I surf the gray, with joy as my guide.
Will I dance with clouds or stumble in muck?
Every twist leads to a fresh stroke of luck!

So here I sail, unsure yet bold,
In this playful gray, my heart's consoled.
With each wave, I find my way,
Navigating life, come what may!

Flickers of Forgotten Futures

In the attic of dreams, dust dances slow,
Past visions of grandeur, with nowhere to go.
A cat with a monocle sips on regret,
While clocks tick in rhythms we barely forget.

Balloons filled with hopes float high in the air,
But one popped with laughter, it's chaos, beware!
A jester in shadows throws pies at the wall,
Painting uncertainty—oh, isn't life a ball?

Navigating through Nebulae

Lost in the cosmos, with ice cream in hand,
I steer my intentions, but where do I land?
A salad of stardust, that tastes just like cheese,
I'm stuck in a quiz with no hint and no keys.

Galaxies spinning like tops gone awry,
I dodge all the comets as they shoot by.
A spaceship of whimsy that squeaks when I steer,
With every wrong turn, I laugh out loud in fear.

Echoes of the Unfamiliar

A riddle of echoes, they swim out of reach,
Like socks in a dryer, all missing their speech.
Whispers of turmoil, tickle my ear,
As I trip over thoughts that I never held dear.

An octopus juggles my hopes with a grin,
While confusion waltzes, it's hard to begin.
Like pancakes that flip and then fall on the floor,
Life's absurdity makes me just laugh even more.

Whirlwinds of Wonder

Caught in a whirlwind of giggles and glee,
I do a cha-cha with uncertainty.
When life throws a curve, I step to the right,
Wearing mismatched socks, what a colorful sight!

The universe chuckles as I dance down the street,
With breadcrumbs of dreams stuck under my feet.
But oh, what a party with chaos in tow,
I'll twirl through the mayhem, just watch me and flow!

When Paths Diverge

Two roads meet, who dares to choose?
One leads to coffee, the other to booze.
Flip a coin, it's quite the thrill,
Heads for laughter, tails for a chill.

A fork in the road, I look around,
Which one leads to lost and found?
Perhaps I'll just wander aimlessly,
With snacks in hand, I feel so free.

Left or right, the signs are bland,
With every step, I take a stand.
It's truly wild, this guessing game,
But hey, at least I'm never lame.

In a world where paths intertwine,
With a twist and turn, I'm feeling fine.
So here's to choices, big and small,
Let's laugh together, and have a ball!

The Mirage of Stability

They say, 'Stay put, you'll find your place.'
But my chair's on wheels, lets me embrace.
I sit, I spin, I glide with glee,
Stability's just a fantasy.

A pot of gold at the rainbow's end,
Or is it just a trick to spend?
With every job post, I sense the joke,
Like choosing soup or getting soaked.

Who needs a plan, it's overrated!
Life's a dance, I'm not frustrated.
Spin me once, or twice if you dare,
My mirage of calm, a breath of fresh air.

So grab your shoes, and dance on the fickle,
For steady life's just a magical tickle.
In this circus of chaos, let's all engage,
With smiles to wear, let's turn the page!

Pulses of the Unseen

The clock ticks loud, but what's the rush?
Maybe I'll nap, just a gentle hush.
Life's wild ride, it's cue to sway,
As time skips along, like a child at play.

Invisible threads, I weave and spin,
What's around the corner? Let the fun begin!
Mysteries lurk, just out of sight,
Balloons pop, and it gives a fright.

A pulse of laughter, then chaos ensues,
Opt for the joy, or watch the blues.
Connections hidden, like socks in the dryer,
Oh, what a game! Life's set on fire.

So dance to the rhythm, let fate decide,
Enjoy the detours, take 'em with pride.
For every beat is a chance to glean,
The laughter in life's vibrant scene.

A Symphony of Unwritten Stories

With every choice, a tale unfolds,
Some are shy, while others are bold.
Characters whirl in a plot twist spree,
Dancing on air, so wild and free.

A whisper of dreams in the chaos near,
Plotting a course, but feels unclear.
Grab a pen, let's draft the unknown,
In lines so quirky, we've never grown.

With madness sprinkled in each refrain,
Life's a novel, with joy and pain.
So turn the pages, don't be a bore,
In this symphony, let's encore more!

Each unwritten line, a chance to delight,
In darkness and humor, we find our light.
So laugh through the tales that stories bring,
For life's silly dance is the sweetest swing.

Variations on a Theme of Chaos

In a world where socks go to hide,
Lack of order is where we reside.
The cat makes a jump, and miss the chair,
While coffee spills show we shouldn't care.

Plans are made with utmost zeal,
Then crumble like a soggy meal.
Today I'll organize my desk,
Or maybe just take a cozy resp.

Dancing through life's little mess,
Who knew chaos could be so blessed?
With laughs and sighs we glide and twist,
Finding joy in that perfect mist.

So raise a glass to the unplanned day,
A toast to the absurd, come what may.
For laughter is the sweetest balm,
In this swirling world so delightfully calm.

The Unruly Nature of Existence

Life's a breakfast of toast and jam,
One side's burnt, and so is the ham.
I reach for the fridge, but find it bare,
Just an odd odor and some stale air.

The sun peeks out, then hides away,
Like a shy cat in the heat of the day.
Why is my umbrella never near?
It's like a clown in a children's fair!

We toss our plans like a salad bowl,
Hoping that fate will take its toll.
Amidst the chaos, we make the call,
To dance on the edge of it all.

So let's giggle in the face of strife,
Play tag with the uncertain knife.
For life's great dance is a curious spin,
A whimsical ride set to begin.

Arcs of Emerging Insights

With every curve, a lesson blooms,
Like socks misplaced in empty rooms.
The more we plan, the more we stray,
Like kids in mud on a sunny day.

The clock ticks loud with a funny song,
It says we're right, but often wrong.
I chase my tail, then laugh out loud,
As the universe joins in the crowd.

A puzzle piece that doesn't fit,
A plan that's gone like a cheeky skit.
But in the mess of this quirky life,
Laughter's the bond, the thread of strife.

So let's embrace the flips and flops,
The peeling paint and the awkward hops.
For every stumble writes a rhyme,
In the slippery dance that is our time.

In the Presence of the Unknown

Staring at the fridge, I ponder deep,
What's that strange thing? A type of creep?
A taco from last week starts to grin,
I swear it just winked—let chaos begin!

The traffic light flickers like a disco rave,
And life feels like a wild, dancy wave.
I wear mismatched shoes, oh what a scene,
Strutting my stuff like a zany queen.

Each twist and turn, a wild surprise,
Like buried treasure or a pie in the eyes.
The rulebook's lost in a cosmic blip,
But who needs order on this fun trip?

So join the party of the unforeseen,
Where nothing is regular, tranquil, or clean.
In the carnival of chaos, we shall play,
With laughter shaping our unsure way.

Whimsy of the Wind

Oh, the wind takes a daily trip,
It dances right atop my lip.
Whistling tunes of absolute glee,
Mocking me, oh can't you see?

It blows hats off with such a charm,
He wraps my scarf like a warm arm.
Skirts swirling in playful pranks,
In his embrace, I give my thanks.

But just when I'm feeling bold,
He flips my plans, or so I'm told.
With every gust, my hopes might sway,
Just like kids on a daring day.

So here we are, in this swirl,
Life's a circus, let it unfurl!
With each breeze a joke awaits,
Uncertainty? It celebrates.

Flashes of Precarious Joy

Life's a ride on a bumpy lane,
Where laughter hides beneath the pain.
A dance on the edge, oh so bizarre,
It feels like I'm juggling with a star.

One minute I'm high, next I'm low,
Like a kite flailing in a show.
With joy that winks and runs away,
It's a game where I often play.

I chase my dreams on a bicycle,
Wobbly while I'm feeling fickle.
If I fall, I'll laugh with grace,
For every scar has a funny face.

So bring on the toss and the spin,
I'll wear my doubts like a silly grin.
In this whirlpool of mishaps, I soar,
Finding joy in the mess we adore.

The Beauty of Broken Roads

There's beauty found in cracks and bends,
Where the path twists but never ends.
A pothole here, a bump or two,
My journey's jolly, how about you?

I stroll with shoes that squeak and slide,
Each misstep a reason to confide.
With laughter echoing down the way,
Uncertainty is my travel play.

Oh, the signs say 'Detour ahead!',
But I'm just grateful, nothing's dead.
Every stumble is a dance, you see,
Make way for joy on the broken spree.

So hand me a map or a blurry guide,
In this chaos, I choose to ride.
Forward I rush, without any load,
For life's quirks make the best of roads.

Murmurs of Distant Horizons

Horizons murmur, whispers float,
Promises wrapped in a silly coat.
They tease with dreams that dance afar,
Like a cat who just chased a star.

In the distance, clouds rearrange,
Crafting tales that feel a bit strange.
They giggle at plans I hold so dear,
Saying, 'Surprise! Just wait right here!'

With every step, a new twist plots,
Life's a game of what you've got.
You skip, you fall, you laugh, you sigh,
A circus act beneath the sky.

So here I stand, with hope ignited,
In this chaos, I'm so excited.
With horizons' whispers leading the way,
I find my fun in each daring day.

The Unwritten Chapters

In the book of life, we scribble and scratch,
What's next in line? A wild mismatch!
Tabs on adventures, sticky notes galore,
Plot twists aplenty, who could ask for more?

The coffee spills, ink drips with flair,
Characters stumble, without any care.
Each blank page waits, with a wink and a cheer,
Unwritten stories, oh dear, oh dear!

A Symphony of Questions

Is it Tuesday or Friday? I forget each week,
Why do socks vanish? Ah, the answers we seek!
Tunes of confusion play loud in my head,
A riddle a minute, oh why must I dread?

With flutes made of doubt, the clarinet's wail,
A cacophony hums, beyond the pale.
Yet laughter erupts, with each quirky note,
For who really knows? Let the chaos float!

Starlight Through the Haze

Under a sky of giggles, we wander and twirl,
Navigating dreams in a dizzying swirl.
Stars blink with laughter, guiding our quest,
Through moments of blunders, we're truly blessed.

The haze veils our eyes, but brightens our grin,
Lost in the fog, yet find ways to win.
With each clumsy step, we dance and we play,
Embracing the chaos, come what may!

The Edge of Reckoning

At the cliff of decisions, do I jump or not?
Will I face a triumph or fall on the spot?
With eyes wide in wonder, I teeter and pause,
Reckoning's call has me laughing because!

The leap might be silly, but oh what a show!
Join me, dear friend, let's take it real slow.
Together we tumble, whether win or loss,
Life's twisted path is our thrilling toss!

Unscripted Moments

In surprise, we find our dance,
With fate's wild twists, we take a chance.
A spilled drink becomes a toast,
We laugh at what we love the most.

Life's script is more of a jive,
Plot twists appear, we come alive.
With every turn, new tales to spin,
Reality's joke, let the game begin!

Each missed cue, a chance to play,
A wrong note brightens up the gray.
In chaos, we weave a tale so grand,
Unscripted moments, oh how they stand!

As we fumble through each day bright,
Clumsy steps, but hearts in flight.
Laughter echoes in the hall,
Let's embrace the tumble, after all.

The Canvas of Conjecture

With splashes bright on canvas wide,
We paint our thoughts, no place to hide.
Each stroke unsure, yet bold and free,
A masterpiece of 'what could be.'

Our brushes dance, they flirt and swoon,
Mixing colors under the moon.
A face of joy, a splash of dread,
Whimsical thoughts swirling in our head.

Surprises come in hues unseen,
Life's abstract in every scene.
A bit of chaos, a touch of grace,
The art of living's a curious race!

We giggle at frames, some crooked, some straight,
In the gallery of chance, we celebrate fate.
Each uncertainty, a shade to embrace,
On our canvas, we paint life's face.

Labyrinth of Lost Directions

In a maze of turns, we laugh and roam,
Chasing signs that lead us home.
"Left or right?" we scratch our heads,
Only to find we've lost our threads!

Each fork in the road, a fresh riddle,
We giggle as we solve each middle.
With upside-down maps and silly grins,
Adventure begins where lostness spins!

Who needs a guide? We make our way,
Through twists and turns, we're here to play.
In this labyrinth, our laughter lingers,
As life tosses us its curveball fingers.

Our compass points in every yet,
Finding joy in every misstep met.
Wanderers at heart, with spirits bold,
In this lost maze, life's treasures unfold!

Fleeting Glimpses of Clarity

In moments brief, clarity shines,
Like sunlight breaking through the pines.
A joke that lands, a wink well-timed,
We pause to laugh, while life's unrhymed.

A silly dance on a crowded street,
Embracing chaos, we find the beat.
The wisdom of folly, it's quite a treat,
In laughter's embrace, we feel complete.

With each strange twist, a lesson gained,
In misadventures, joy's sustained.
We see the truth in a comical slip,
Life's wacky ride, we take a trip!

So here's to those flashes of light,
In all the confusion, we play the knight.
With laughter our shield, we boldly roam,
Finding clarity in the chaos, our home.

Rhythms of a Restless Heart

My heart beats like a drum, oh so wild,
Each thump a secret, each pause a child.
I dance to the chaos, twirl in dismay,
In this funny waltz of a topsy-turvy ballet.

When plans fall apart like a soggy breeze,
I laugh with the mischief of fallen leaves.
The universe chuckles, this life's all a jest,
One big circus act, and I'm part of the quest.

I aim for the stars but land in a pie,
A face full of cream, oh my, oh my!
Yet there's joy in the slip, a slip of the shoe,
In the dance of the dreams, the absurd is true.

So here's to the rhythms that toss me around,
I'll jiggle and groove, for laughter's profound.
With each beat I stumble, a life's little spree,
It's a humorous heart that will always be free.

Borders of the Unknown

Peeking past the fence of a world unclear,
I search for the answers, but they just disappear.
With a map full of doodles and a compass that spins,
I'm lost in the riddle, the game that life wins.

Every corner I turn brings a fresh pair of socks,
Though they're mismatched, I smile—just my paradox.
A plan made in haste can unravel like yarn,
But laughter's a gift from the cosmic sea barn.

Uncharted waters, a boat made of goo,
I navigate whimsies, like wading through stew.
The borders are blurry; I trip on my fate,
But the unknown is friendly, just watch out for bait!

With quirky surprises around every bend,
I'll toast to the chaos, my very good friend.
In this realm of the weird, I'm keen for the ride,
For life's vibrant colors are joyously wide.

Chimeras of Assurance

I woke up this morning, all ready to strive,
Yet the coffee was cold—it barely survived!
Promises made by the universe, WHOA,
It's a prankster indeed, setting me up for a show.

Each attempt at control feels just like a dream,
An illusion like shadows that laugh and scream.
I juggle my worries like pies in midair,
Watch them all splatter—what a slapstick affair!

The safety I crave is a marshmallow ghost,
It crumbles and giggles, a soft-hearted boast.
Surety winks from its comfy recline,
While I trip on my shoelace, sipping on brine.

Yet I wear a fine smile like a hat on a cat,
With chimeras of certainty dancing like that.
For in the absurd, there's beauty to find,
A carnival world—where I'm one of a kind.

The Crucible of Transformation

Life's like a blender with a faulty switch,
It whirls and it twirls, making me rich.
I toss in my dreams, and what do I get?
A smoothie of chaos, a funny vignette!

One day I'm a lion, next day a flea,
Mixing up personas like a recipe spree.
With laughter as spice, I sauté my doubts,
In this kitchen of change, there's no place for pouts.

The ups and the downs like a see-saw at play,
Each wobble a giggle, come join in the fray!
If life hands you lemons, just make it a show,
A citrusy dance with a zesty glow.

So here's to the potions we brew every day,
For each ripple and twist brings a new chance to sway.
With whimsical shadows, I'm ready to shine,
In this crucible's magic, I find what is mine.

The Driftwood's Journey

On a riverbank, driftwood lays,
Wonders lost in sunlit rays.
It dreams of oceans wide and grand,
But floats on currents, unmapped land.

A twig with thoughts of being proud,
Yet finds itself beneath the cloud.
With each wave, it takes a spin,
Always guessing where it's been.

It wishes for a life of flair,
Not just debris in the air.
But hey, it laughs in wooden tones,
As petals dance, it finds its bones.

So here it drifts, in waters deep,
Waving at all who dare to peek.
For in its journey, fun unfolds,
In every twist, a tale retold.

Mosaic of Unforeseen Choices

A puzzle box with missing parts,
Decisions made with eager hearts.
Each piece, a laugh, a little squint,
A mismatched look, a cheeky hint.

Stumbling blind on a game of chance,
Awkward moves, a clumsy dance.
Who knew wrong turns could feel so bright,
When every flub's a laugh at night?

Painted tiles with wobbly lines,
Life's stitching paths that tease and twine.
We build our dreams from bits and bobs,
And laugh at life's whimsical jabs.

In this crazy quilt, we're alive,
Embracing chaos, we thrive and strive.
So let's patchwork joy and cheer,
For in the mess, there's fun, my dear!

Hues of Hope and Hesitation

A palette dips in colors bright,
With strokes that dance and twist in light.
But wait! The brush can paint it wrong,
Each swirl a giggle, each line a song.

With every hue, a choice appears,
Some are bold, while others clear.
The painter smiles, a playful grin,
Will it be bliss, or just a spin?

Shades of cheer and paints of dread,
On canvas, we've both laughed and bled.
A splotch of fate on a blank space,
Turns into joy; oh, what a race!

Brush strokes blend, as doubts arise,
Yet here we stand, with hopeful eyes.
In every splatter, life's delight,
A masterpiece of jest and light.

The Hourglass of Hesitance

Sand slips down this wobbly tower,
Ticking softly, bringing power.
Yet lo! The grains do pause and play,
Like thoughts we keep, then toss away.

An hourglass of "what's the plan?",
Will I be first, or just a fan?
Each grain a chuckle, tipped and turned,
In every wait, a lesson learned.

Counting moments with a whim,
As visions blur, the glass grows dim.
A gentle nudge, a pinch of fate,
Yet my feet say, "Better wait!"

But while I sit, the laughter flows,
In hesitant beats, as suspense grows.
So here I am, both lost and found,
In this hourglass, let joy abound.

Unseen Pathways Before Me

In slippers worn and coffee brewed,
I wonder where the day will lead.
With socks that clash and plans askew,
My breakfast toast is often freed.

Each step I take, a question flares,
Is it a win, or just routine?
The cat looks on with knowing stares,
As I debate what clothes to glean.

The garden needs some weeding done,
Yet I? I'd rather watch the sun.
Am I the tortoise, swift but sly?
Or hare who dreams and passes by?

But then I laugh and take a chance,
Life's dance can be a funny trance.

Echoes of Ambiguity

What's for dinner? Let's just guess,
Leftovers, pizza—who knows best?
The fridge is full of options stark,
Yet all I see? A lonely shark.

Should I take risks or play it safe?
The choices here are quite a waif.
Like socks that go their separate ways,
Confusion reigns in humorous ways.

Shall I embrace my quirky fate,
Or switch it up and tempt the plate?
The barista smiles, but what's their cue?
Do they serve tea or something new?

Oh laughter wins, it's plain to see,
In life's big game, we're all just free.

Dancing on the Edge of Doubt

Tiptoe through a world unknown,
On wobbly paths we're not alone.
With smiles that hide our tremoring feet,
We jump and twirl to an offbeat beat.

Oh, fortune smiles or frowns, I say,
Should I wear this hat today?
With layers thick and choices wide,
I chase the whims like a kite in the tide.

A leap of faith, a balmy breeze,
Where is that certainty I seek to seize?
I laugh aloud at all my fears,
While pouring out confetti cheers.

So let us dance, oh wily fate,
With futures bright, we'll navigate!

Fragments of a Shattered Compass

In a world where signs confuse,
I chase the north, it feels like a ruse.
The map's all inked, with doodles and stars,
Who knew I'd get lost behind these bars?

My compass spins, it leads me astray,
Is that a landmark? Or just a café?
I asked for direction, got a goofy grin,
Now I'm contemplating where to begin!

With every turn, I find a new delight,
A taco truck here, a cat in sight.
The journey's a ride, albeit unsure,
These fragments of life make my heart pure!

Delicate Dances with Destiny

I twirl with fate in oversized shoes,
Two left feet, and some questionable moves.
Destiny winks and trips me along,
I'm laughing and groaning to my own song.

A tango with chance, so clumsy yet sweet,
Spilling my drink on a stranger's seat.
With every misstep, I stumble and find,
A giggle that lingers, distractions unwind.

Sometimes we leap, sometimes we fall,
It's all part of dancing, after all!
The rhythm of chaos keeps pulling me near,
Each step is uncertain, yet I persevere!

Uncharted Waters of Emotion

I set sail on a sea of unknown waves,
My heart's the vessel, it's far from brave.
The anchor's missing, adrift in a swirl,
A shark just winked, oh boy, what a whirl!

The tides of joy and sadness collide,
I navigate chaos, with giggles I ride.
Storm clouds chuckle, then clear the way,
Uncharted waters, come what may!

Charts drawn in crayon, they wobble and sway,
I steer my heart-boat, come join in the play!
With every wave, a quirk, a surprise,
Who knew uncertainty could wear such nice ties?

Reflections in a Broken Mirror

I gaze into shards that fracture and dance,
My image is warped, not a chance for romance.
Pixels of laughter and grains of my fears,
I chuckle at how I appear through the years.

This mirror's a puzzle, with pieces askew,
Each glimpse a reminder of something anew.
Mismatched reflections, but oh such a show!
I laugh at the creature in porcelain glow.

A smile at myself, though I'm twisted and bent,
No need for perfection, just a hint of intent.
Life is a carnival, wild and unclear,
And I'm just a jester, giving joy a cheer!

Winters of Indecision

In winter's chill, I can't decide,
Whether to wear gloves or hide.
Should I sip tea or grab a snack?
Life's frosty choices, I can't take back.

Snowflakes fall, and thoughts collide,
Should I stay in or take a ride?
Boots or slippers? Don't make me choose!
In every moment, I just might lose.

The heater's on, but so are my doubts,
Should I change plans, as winter shouts?
Hot cocoa calls, yet I'm still unsure,
As bleak days fade, the urge to explore.

So here I sit all wrapped up tight,
In a world of choices, laughing at fright.
With fuzzy socks and a goofy grin,
I might just roll the dice and spin!

Gentle Murmurs of Change

The world around me starts to sway,
Should I go bold or just delay?
Like leaves that dance, my heart's unclear,
Do I move forward or just stay here?

The breeze whispers secrets in my ear,
What's that you say? Could it be fear?
Should I laugh loud or shed a tear?
Life's playful jest, always sincere.

Gentle nudges from fate's soft hand,
Push me to take that leap and stand.
But what if I trip and fall on my face?
Now that would add a twist to the chase!

With every chuckle at life's weird game,
I find that uncertainty's never the same.
In a world of giggles, I'll stumble along,
As change sings a merry little song.

The Labyrinth of Life

In the maze I find uncertainty's frame,
Wandering paths, they're never the same.
Should I take a left or a right?
Endless confusion, oh what a sight!

Walls whisper doubts I can't outrun,
Choices like shadows, never much fun.
Turn around, re-trace my stride,
In this labyrinth, no place to hide.

With twists and turns, my head starts to spin,
Should I go forward or dare to begin?
The map I drew looks like a doodle,
Navigating life can be quite a riddle.

Though laughter echoes through every bend,
I'll dance through the maze, and make it my friend.
For giggles and grins are my guiding light,
In this wild labyrinth, I'll find my delight!

Sparkles of Uncertainty

In a world that twinkles with doubt's bright spark,
I ask myself, 'Is it light or just dark?'
Glitters of chaos in every new plan,
Will I be the hero, or just a fan?

Life's like confetti tossed in the air,
Should I catch some or just stand and stare?
Those sparkles whisper, 'Join in the fun!'
But which one's the best? Oh, I'm on the run!

A dance with fate, unsure of the beat,
Should I step left, or skip to the street?
With each goofy twirl, I wobble with glee,
Uncertainty's rhythm is just right for me.

So bring on the glitter, the mishaps galore,
With laughter in waves, I'll always want more.
For in the dance of life, I'll twirl and whirl,
With sparkles of humor, I'll take on the world!

The Map of Misadventures

With directions scribbled in pen,
I found myself lost again.
GPS said, 'Turn right, don't roam!'
But I ended up far from home.

A treasure marked with an X so bold,
Led to a scene both strange and cold.
I dug for gold, found a shoe,
Now it's my only clue to pursue.

Every detour's a laugh, I confess,
Map in hand, yet I still am a mess.
At the crossroads of fate and chance,
I dance with my steps, a clumsy prance.

Despite the errors that come my way,
Every moment's a whimsied play.
With each turn, I tease and jest,
For getting lost? It's all a quest!

Tentative Steps in Twilight

As daylight fades, I tiptoe near,
With shadows lurking, I show no fear.
One step forward, then two back,
Like a chicken in a game, I'm on track.

In twilight's hug, uncertainty thrives,
I dance with thoughts, oh how it jives!
Will the moonlight guide me home?
Or will I trip? Oh, how I'd groan!

Each crack in pavement makes me squeal,
What's that sound? A squeaky wheel!
With laughter ringing, I fear not the dark,
These steps might lead to something stark.

Though the night is full of snares,
I'll laugh with whimsy; everyone stares.
For in this twilight, I lose all grace,
But I shuffle and giggle, it's my happy place!

The Veil of Tomorrow's Dreams

I peek through the veil, but what do I see?
A llama in slippers, sipping green tea.
What a curious sight—what does it mean?
Life's tapestry woven with threads unforeseen.

Tomorrow's a riddle wrapped in a bow,
With every guess, the plot thickens, you know.
Will I find bliss or a pie in the face?
Oh, laughter brings joy, I'll embrace the chase.

Blurred visions dance in the flurry of fate,
Some are delightful, while others lay bait.
I'll wear my disguise—an old paper hat,
Ready for anything, including a chat!

Dreams like balloons float over my head,
What's next in this circus? I'm joyfully led.
As the veil sways, it teases and gleams,
In this carnival of odd, I'll ride on my dreams!

Chasing Elusive Truths

With a net made of questions, I chase the divine,
But truths are like butterflies, dancing in line.
I leap and I tumble, my effort absurd,
Each time I get close, they flutter, unheard.

Truth's in a cornfield, or so they say,
I'm lost in the maze, munching on hay.
Should I follow the crows that cackle and tease?
Or rely on the breeze, which whispers with ease?

In pursuit of the facts, I find witty lies,
Like 'cheese-eating mice' or 'dogs in disguise.'
With laughter as my compass, I wander around,
In the chase of the truth, it's jesting I've found.

So here I remain, with a smirk and a grin,
For elusive truths are a fun place to spin.
With each playful chase, I twirl and I sing,
In the comedy of life, I'm embracing the fling!

www.ingramcontent.com/pod-product-compliance
Lightning Source LLC
Chambersburg PA
CBHW071854160426
43209CB00003B/551